MW01257713

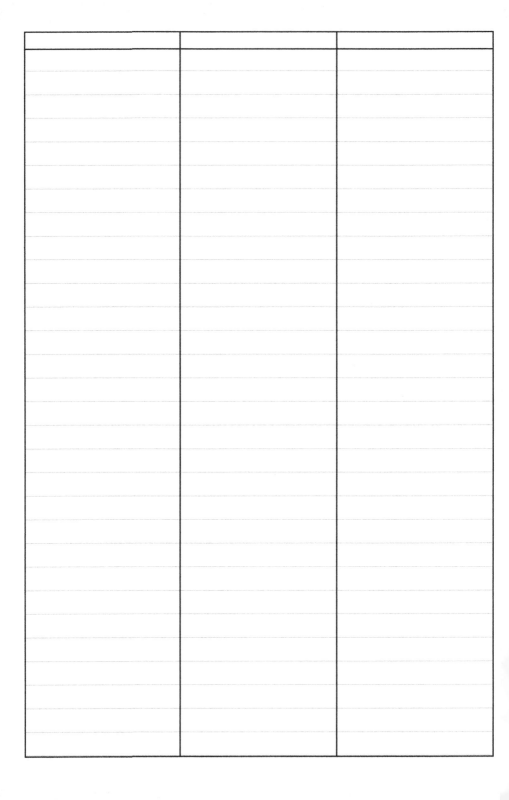

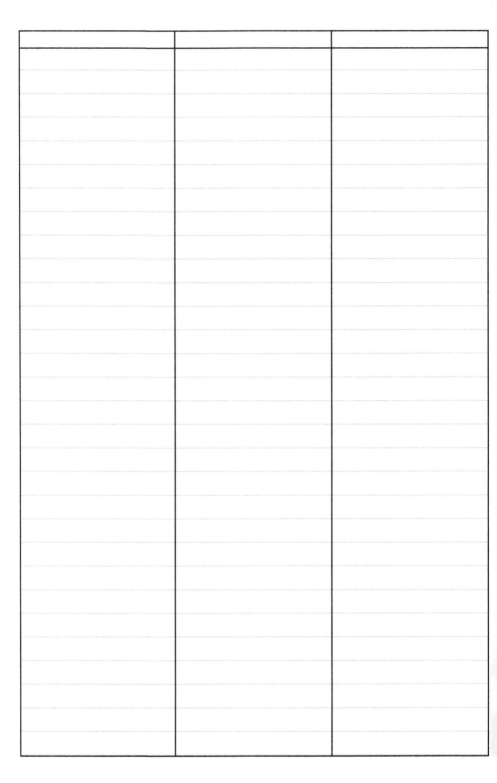

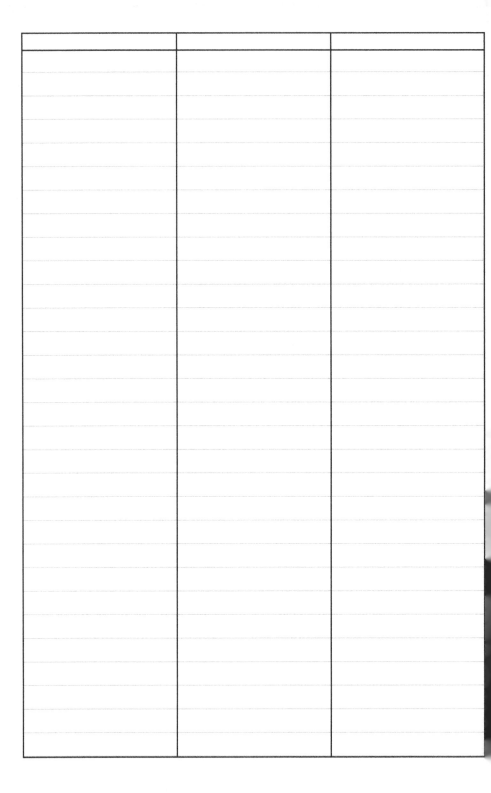

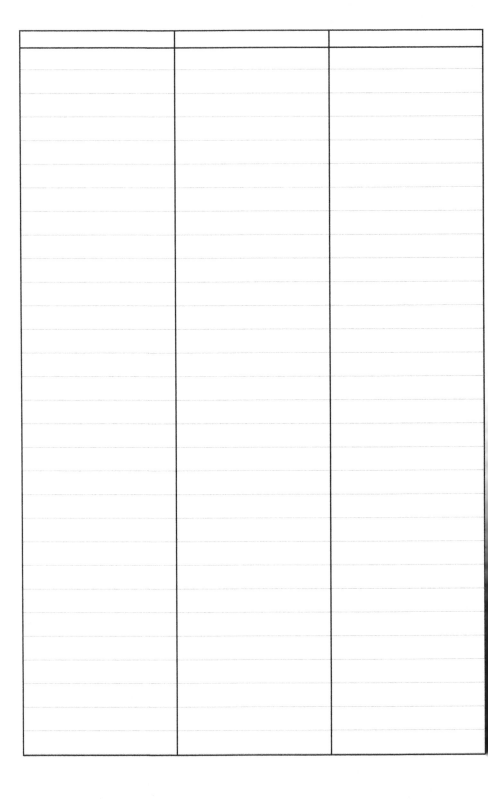

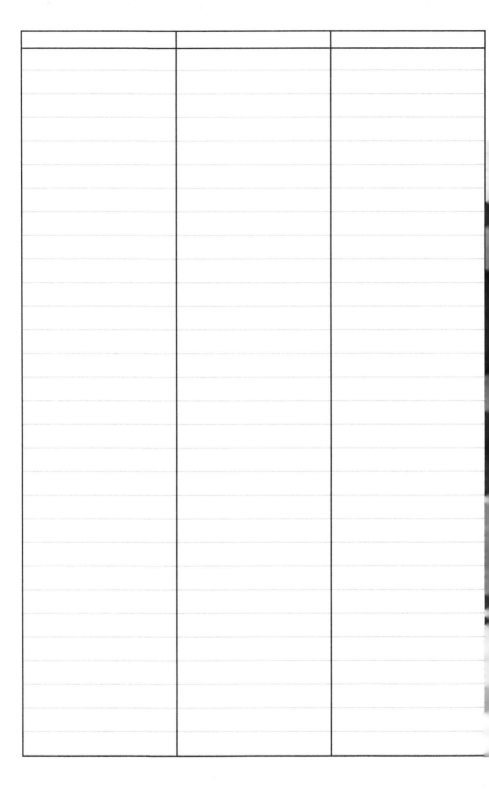

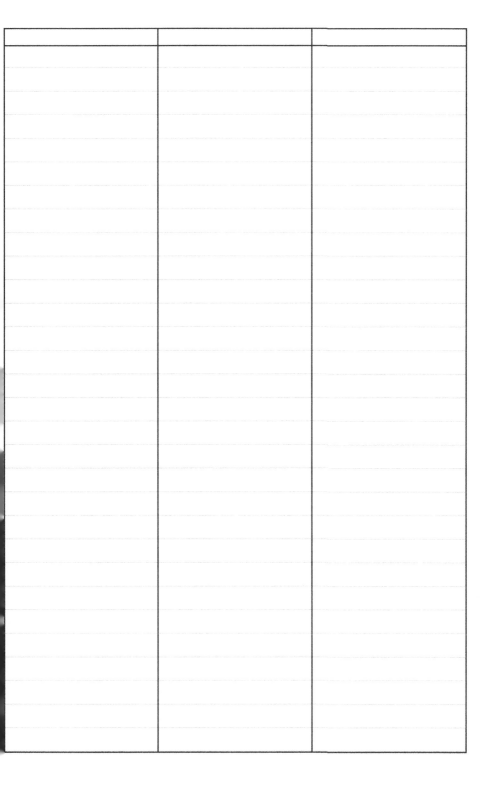

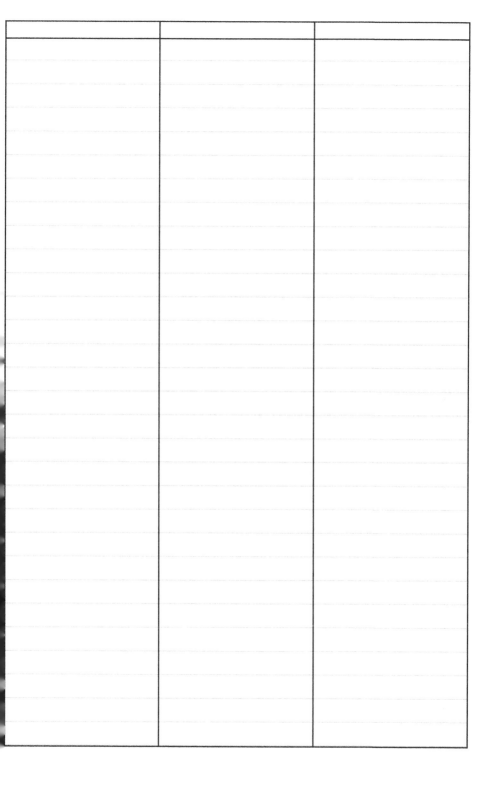

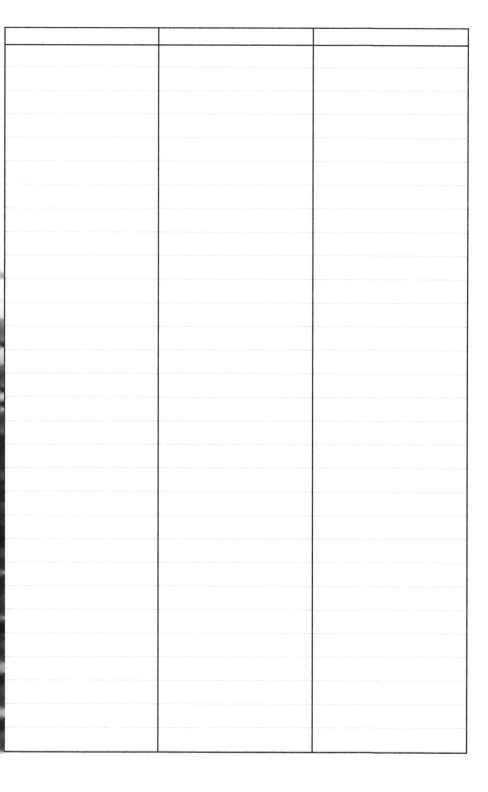

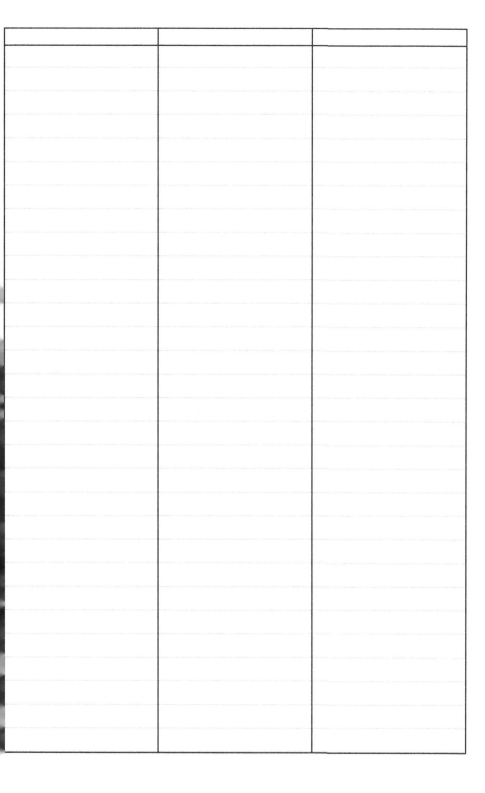

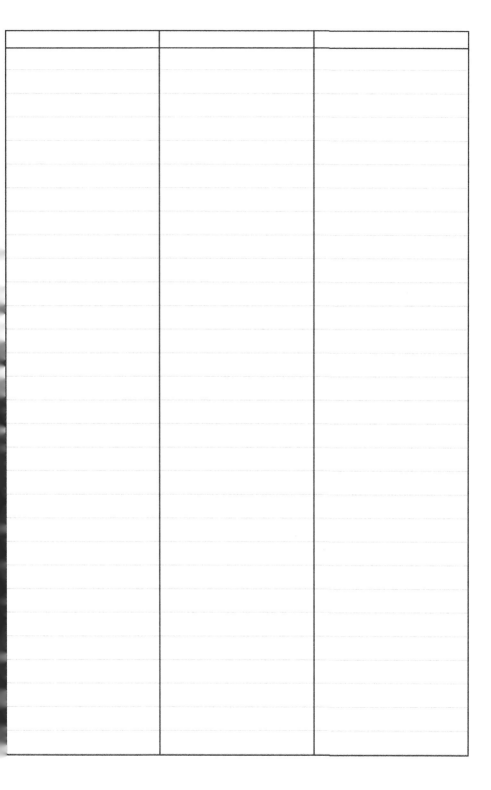

Made in the USA
Las Vegas, NV
02 May 2024

89432094R00069